Eddy's Nutty Adventure

illustrated by
Daniel Wlodarski

Written by
Vida Atefy

Eddy's Nutty Adventure
Written by Vida Atefy
Typesetting, formatting and
illustrated by Daniel Wlodarski
Copyright Vida Atefy ©
ISBN number: 978-1-0689270-0-3

Printed by BookBaby
Edition first
Queensville 2024

EDdY'S
Nutty Adventure

illustrated by
Daniel Wlodarski

Written by
Vida Atefy

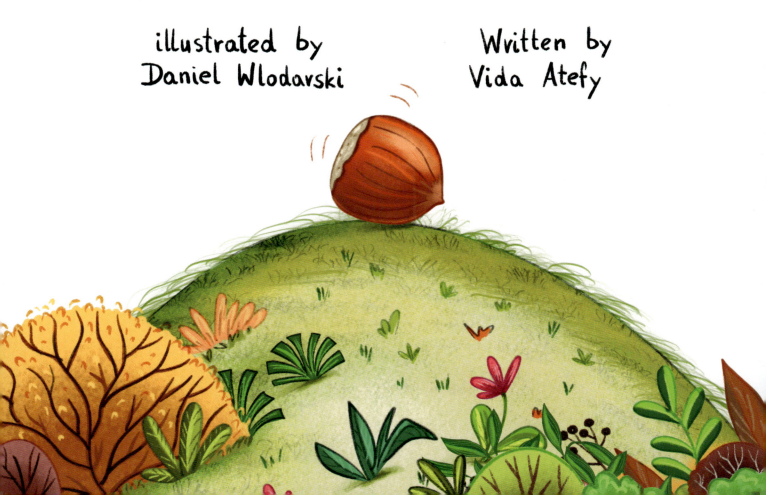

In a green forest, there lived
a small squirrel named Eddy.

He loved to play

and **jump** in the trees.

One day, Eddy saw a shiny hazelnut.

He wanted to catch it.

That nut will be mine!

he said.

But the nut
fell from
the tree...

...and rolled away.

Eddy ran after it.

Wait for me, nut!

he called.

Eddy chased the nut through the forest.
He met Bella the Butterfly.
I'll help you she said.

They found the nut on a hill.
But oh no!
It rolled down the hill.

Eddy, ran fast after it.

At the bottom of the hill, Eddy met Rosie the Rabbit.
The nut went that way
said Rosie.

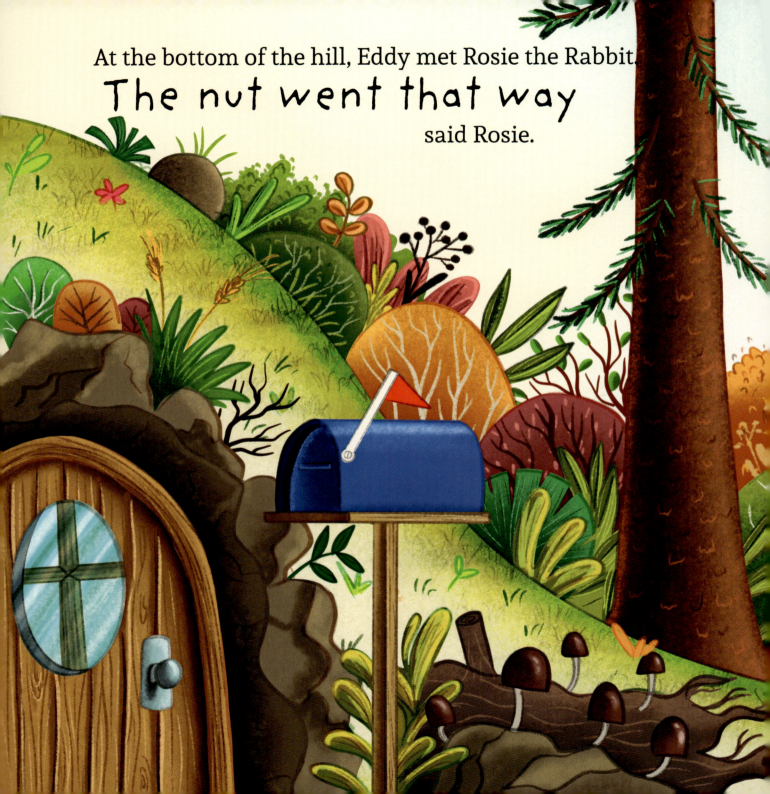

Eddy and Rosie found the nut by a river.
It was about to fall in! **Oh no!** said Eddy.

Just then, Ben the Beaver
pushed the nut back to the shore.

Eddy catches the nut.

He was happy and thanked all his new friends.

Eddy shared the nut with Bella, Rosie, and Ben.
They all enjoyed it together.

Eddy felt happy to have friends in the forest.

Friends are better than nuts

he giggled.

Every day, Eddy and his friends played together.

And sometimes, they found more nuts!